TOPICS
IN HOME
ECONOMICS

FOOD INVESTIGATIONS

Barbara Wynn

Oxford University Press

Oxford University Press, Walton Street, Oxford OX2 6DP

Oxford   New York   Toronto
Delhi   Bombay   Calcutta   Madras   Karachi
Petaling Jaya   Singapore   Hong Kong   Tokyo
Nairobi   Dar es Salaam   Cape Town
Melbourne   Auckland

and associated companies in
Beirut   Ibadan   Berlin   Nicosia

Oxford is a trade mark of Oxford University Press

© B. Wynn 1986
Reprinted 1987 (twice)
ISBN 0 19 832722 6

Acknowledgements

Designed by Raynor Design.

Illustrations are by Gecko Ltd., Jon Riley, Kate Simunek.

Cover illustration is by Barbara Mullarney-Wright.

The publisher would like to thank the following for permission to reproduce their photographs:

Hill and Knowlton p.18; Rob Judges p.12, p.20, p.27 (top), p.42, p.43, p.45, p.47, p.51; Queen Elizabeth College p.27 (bottom left and right), p.30.

The author would like to thank the staff at Didcot Girls School for their help, and David Wynn for his encouragement.

Abbreviations used

g	gram
cm	centimetre
ml	millilitre
SR	self-raising
°C	degrees Celsius
°F	degrees Farenheit
tbsp	tablespoon
tsp	teaspoon

The experiment is best done in pairs

The work in the experiment should be shared out between different members of the class.

Collect together equipment or ingredients.

Phototypeset by Tradespools Limited, Frome, Somerset, England
Printed in Great Britain by Scotprint Limited, Musselburgh, Scotland.

Contents

For the teacher   4
For pupils   6
How to write up an experiment   7

Section 1   Investigations and projects

How to weigh and measure   8
Recipe costing with a calculator   9
Project work   10
How to do a simple survey   12
School meals survey   14
Shopping surveys   15
Can you remember what you ate?   16
Cheese tasting   18
Milk tasting   19
Food labels and additives (1)   20
Food labels and additives (2)   22
Can I trust the information?   24

Section 2   Basic foods and mixtures

Plant cells   26
Tests with flour   28
Heating starch and sugar   30
Effect of heat on protein food (1)   32
Effect of heat on protein food (2)   34
Mixtures in foods   36
Making dairy foods   38

Section 3   Equipment, and experimental cookery

Choosing and using equipment   40
Evaluating large equipment   42
Whisking egg whites   44
Cooking eggs   46
Making cakes   48
Pastry making   50
What does yeast need to grow?   52
Preserving apples   54
Convenience foods   56

Section 4   Simple tests with food

Testing food for acidity   58
Food tests on yogurt and milk   60
Tests for vitamin C, starch, and fat   62

Index   64

For the teacher

This book uses an experimental approach to food so that pupils can investigate and understand what happens to food when it is prepared and cooked.

Teachers often wish to encourage an experimental approach to Home Economics but do not have the time for a whole course or even whole lessons on experimental work. This book will enable teachers to develop investigative and experimental skills even when time is short.

The book is aimed particularly at pupils in the first few years of secondary schools, but there are many experiments and ideas that will be useful for older pupils and for GCSE classes. The ideas about organizing projects have proved useful for both younger and older pupils.

There are four main sections in the book.

1 **Investigations and projects** where pupils are encouraged to undertake a wide range of individual and group activities which do not involve cooking.
2 **Basic foods and mixtures** where pupils can investigate basic foods and the changes which occur in cooking.
3 **Equipment and experimental cookery.** Some basic methods and techniques are investigated in this section.
4 **Simple tests with food.** These involve the use of some chemicals and science equipment.

The book contains information and instructions for experiments. Ideas for recording results are included as well as questions, further work, and suggestions for the extension of the experiments.

The experiments are designed for classroom use within the Home Economics department. Few require the use of a laboratory or specialist equipment, apart from test tubes. Many of the experiments could also be tried at home.

Pupils should be able to make decisions about the choice of recipes, food, and equipment based on their knowledge and experience of this work. The pupils will also be helped to apply scientific techniques to familiar situations.

The processes and skills involved in doing this work are as important as the results. Pupils are helped to observe and measure, to analyse and interpret, to assess and consider what is relevant, to test and to check, then to discuss and record their work as well as evaluating the results.

Pupils are encouraged to develop their own questioning approach and to design their own experimental work.

The book can be tackled in any order according to the needs of the pupils and interests and concerns of the teacher.

Practical suggestions

Most of the experiments can be carried out quickly and could be fitted into a practical or theory lesson covering other related areas of work.

The symbol 👥 is used to indicate experiments that are best done in pairs or small groups.

In the experiments such as pastry or cake making where work is to be shared out between different members of the class, the sections of work are clearly divided up and the teacher will need to allocate sections to individuals, pairs, or groups as required. These experiments tend to be longer and may take a single or double lesson. They are marked with the symbol 👥👥.

For group experiments it would be useful for the teacher to prepare a summary of each results chart on the blackboard, or on an overhead projector transparency, for pupils to fill in as they complete their section of the work.

Pupils should not have any difficulty in understanding the results of their experiments but the help of the teacher may be needed in interpreting them and applying the knowledge gained to future practical work. Pupils, especially those who have had some experience of experimental work, may be able to develop their conclusions in group discussions.

Most of the experiments involve the production of food which can be used up in suitable dishes or eaten after the experiment. Where the food is not to be consumed this is made clear in the instructions and very small quantities are used in order to keep costs down.

Basic Home Economics equipment is not included in the equipment list unless it is likely to be needed quickly in the middle of an experiment. Long lists of equipment serve only to confuse pupils.

In most cases simple items such as jam jars can be used instead of laboratory equipment. A supply of test tubes will be necessary, but it is possible that other items (which are usually optional) might be borrowed from a school Science department if not available in the Home Economics department. A microscope would be particularly useful.

Coordination of this work with the Science department may help pupils to transfer and apply their knowledge more widely.

For pupils

Experiments can help you to understand what happens when you prepare and cook food. When you have completed the experiments in this book you should have a better understanding of many of the recipes that you use. Once you understand how a recipe works then you can change it and still get good results.

This book also gives you ideas on how to find things out from other people. These methods of working will be useful to you in many different subjects at school.

If you haven't time to carry out all the experiments in school, some of them could be carried out at home.

In most of these experiments you will need to work with other people. Share the work fairly. Always aim to work as part of a team, helping one another and using your time wisely.

Basic rules for any experiment

1 Only change one thing at a time or you will not know what has happened in your experiment.

You need a **control** or 'basic recipe' to compare with your other results. If you do not have a control it is difficult to understand your results. You have probably used a control in science experiments too.

2 It is usually best to repeat experiments several times so that you can be sure of the results. If you haven't time to do this in class make sure that your work is as accurate as possible.

3 Always *listen* carefully to any instructions that you are given by your teacher. *Read* the instructions in this book carefully too.

4 Work in a clean and safe way. Follow the basic rules that you have learned about working in a kitchen, and about working in a laboratory.

How to write up an experiment

It is important to keep a written record of your experiments so that you can remember what you did and refer to your results when you are cooking. Other people in the class might also need your results to compare with their own. It is impossible to remember the details of this type of work unless you write about it at the time. You need to explain what you did, what happened and what it all means.

One way to write up an experiment is like this:

Aim What you want to find out.
Method Brief explanation of how you did the experiment.
Results A results chart is very important to let you see and compare all your results easily. Here is an example.

\multicolumn{6}{c}{The effect of extra sugar in cake recipes}
Method used	Size and shape	Appearance	Taste	Texture	Comments
1 control cake	well risen— size 3 cm in centre 2½ cm at edges	golden brown	moist	light	a good result
2 extra sugar	cake sank in middle 1 cm in centre 2 cm at edges	burnt at edges	sticky, harder edges, too sweet	heavy and sticky	a very poor result

You do not have to use the results charts shown in the book. You can use your own results charts if you wish. Remember to write a heading for any results chart.

Conclusions There is little point in doing an experiment unless you learn something from it. The conclusion should show what you have learned. It should be a summary of the main things that have happened. It is also useful to explain how you could use this information when cooking.

For example if you found that too much sugar resulted in poor cakes, then your conclusion should state that it is important to weigh sugar carefully when making cakes and it should also explain why. If you found that your control cake gave the best results, then your conclusion might suggest that this appears to be a good recipe to follow.

Section 1
Investigations and projects

How to weigh and measure

It is important to know how to measure and weigh with and without scales.

measuring jug
empty milk bottle
water
flour
tablespoon
set of scales

Find out and write down your results

1 How many tablespoons of water measure 50 ml?
2 How many millilitres does a milk bottle hold?
3 What are the largest and smallest volumes that your measuring jug will measure?
4 Draw the pair of scales that you have been given. Show the measurements on the scale and the type of weights used.
5 What are the largest and smallest weights that can be measured on your scales?
6 What is the weight of one rounded tablespoon of flour?
7 What is the weight of one level tablespoon of flour?

Quiz

1 How many rounded tablespoons of flour would weigh 50 g?
   a 2   b 4   c 8   d 2½
2 Approximately how much of a milk bottle's contents would be needed to measure 250 ml?
   a ½ bottle   b ¼ bottle   c 2 bottles   d 1 bottle
3 What would be the weight of each of these sections in a standard tub or packet of margarine?
   a 200 g   b 25 g   c 10 g   d 50 g
4 How many grams in a kilogram?
   a 100   b 10   c 1000   d 10000
5 How many millilitres in a litre?
   a 500   b 1000   c 100   d 25

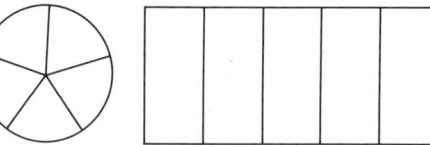

Answers 1a 2a 3d 4c 5b

Recipe costing with a calculator

It is often useful to know the cost of different recipes. Here is an easy example, try working it out in your head first.

If 10 apples cost 50p what is the cost of one apple?

Obviously the answer is 5p. How did you work it out? You divided the cost by the number of apples so 1 apple costs 50÷10=5p

Now work out the cost of 350 g of sugar from a packet which weighs 1 kg (1000 g) and costs 50p. You can use a calculator.
If 1000 g costs 50p, then 1 g must cost 50÷1000=0.05p
So 350 g must cost 0.05×350= 17.5p

The cost of 350 g of this sugar is therefore 18p to the nearest p.

Summary

To work out the cost of ingredients do these sums:

cost of whole packet, tin or total cost of items in **pence**	÷	total weight of packet, tin or items **in grams**
	=	first answer

This gives you the cost of 1 g of ingredients. Then:

first answer	×	the weight of ingredients you used **in grams**	=	your cost

This gives you the cost of the weight of ingredients you used. Always try to work out sums in your head before you use your calculator.

Quiz

Work out the answers to these questions. (Work to the nearest 1p so 2.4p will equal 2p, 3.9p and 4.1p will each equal 4p.)

If 1 kg (1000 g) sugar costs 60p what is the cost of
1 150 g   a 10p   b 5p   c 25p   d 9p
2 25 g   a 2p   b 1p   c 7p   d 5p

If 1½ kg flour (1500 g) costs 63p what is the cost of:
3 100 g   a 30p   b 3p   c 4p   d 10p
4 75 g   a 6p   b 3p   c 2p   d 15p

Answers 1d 2a 3c 4b

Project work

Project work can be fun. You can learn a lot from it. Follow these steps to help you.

Plan

Choose a topic, if one has not been chosen for you. List what you know about it already. Decide what else you will need to find out. Work out how best to collect your information.

Collect information

Visit libraries in school and near home. Write away for information, for example to manufacturers. Ask people for help (librarians, teachers, family or friends). Include lots of different ideas such as: interviews, surveys, experiments, pictures and diagrams, reports of visits and outings—as well as information from books!

Choose and use information

Check that the books are up to date, that they contain useful information and that you can understand them.
Use contents pages and indexes to help you.
Pick out the most important parts. *Do not copy.* Write in your own words and make sure you can understand what you have written.
Make a list of titles and authors of books and leaflets that you use. This list is your **bibliography** and should be put at the back of your project.

Present in an interesting way

Always label and explain any diagrams, pictures, graphs or tables of results. This information looks good when mounted on plain or coloured paper. Present your work using a variety of different approaches. Put the information in a sensible order. Divide your work into sections or chapters if you wish.

Evaluate your project

This means working out its value. What have you learned? Do you have any new skills? How could you improve your work? Include these points in your conclusion.

One good way to set out your project is like this:

Page 1
TITLE

Page 2
CONTENTS
- A list of the main topics covered and page numbers if needed.

Page 3
INTRODUCTION
- Say why you have chosen this topic, what you hope to find out, and how you will obtain your information.

Page 4 onwards
PROJECT
- Include lots of your own ideas. Show that you have found out things for yourself in many different ways.

At the end
CONCLUSION
- Summary of your main points. What you have learned and how your work might be useful to you. Evaluate your work, and the methods you have used to collect information.

Last page
BIBLIOGRAPHY
- List all the books and leaflets used.

What the teacher is looking for in your project

It is original and not just copied. It is your work.

It is interesting, lively and well thought-out.

You have included lots of different ideas and collected your information in a variety of ways.

It is easy to read and attractively presented.

Your conclusion explains clearly what you have found out.

You have evaluated your work.

You have really thought about your work and taken trouble with it.

How to do a simple survey

You can often find out a lot about a topic you are studying by carrying out a survey and studying the answers that people give you.

Here are the stages that you need to go through. An example of one survey is given to help you to plan your own work.

1 **Work out what you want to know**

   For example you may wish to find out about the popularity of different breakfast cereals.

2 **Write out your question or questions**

   The questions must be clear and easy to understand. Don't make them too long or ask too many questions. For example you might just ask 'which cereal do you like best?'

3 **Decide whom to question**

   The more people you ask, the more meaningful your results, but your time will probably be short. You could ask members of your class at school, your neighbours or local shoppers.

4 **Before you start**

   Make sure that you have read the points above and know what you are doing.

5 **Ask people your questions**

   Write down their replies.
   A clip-board, paper and pencil will help.

6 Write up your results

a Bar charts (or block graphs) are a good way to show the results of your survey. Don't forget to label them and give a title.

b You may prefer to use a pie-chart. You draw a circle and divide it up in proportion to your results. The results shown in the block graph and the pie chart are the same. You may have learned how to do pie charts in your maths lessons. Your teacher will show you how to do it if you don't know, as this method is more difficult.

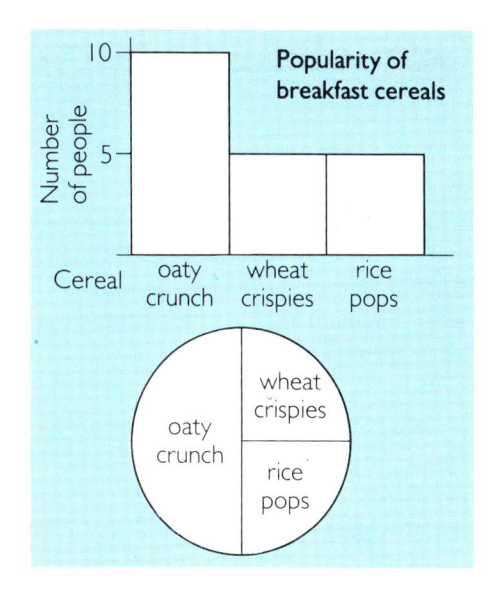

c Write a summary of the main points of your study and write your conclusions. Say what you have found out and try to explain your results. Say how you could have improved the work. Be careful not to suggest that the results given to you by a few people apply to everyone.

Further work

1 Carry out a survey on school meals or on shopping as suggested on the next page. Some other ideas for surveys are:

Labour-saving machines in the home
You could find out how many people of those you question own a:
a washing machine   b vacuum cleaner   c dish washer
d microwave cooker   e food processor

Safety
You could find out how many people of those you question have a fire extinguisher in their homes.
You might also try to find out how much people know about safety.

Diet and health
You could question people about the foods they eat.
You could also find out how much exercise they take each day.
For example you could find out:
a how many miles they walk or cycle each day
b how many minutes they spend playing sport
c how many minutes they spend doing exercises

2 Find out what a **random sample** is. Why is this method of sampling better than the method that you used or will use?

School meals survey

Ask your school meals supervisor if you can conduct a survey on the school meals and/or packed meals chosen by pupils at your school. Stand where you can see what pupils have chosen to eat and quickly write down what is included in 10 or 20 meals as they come past you (these numbers make it easier to work out your results). Number each meal you see. If you cannot write down every meal fast enough, then write down alternate meals.

Now write up your results. First group the foods together, e.g. fried foods, sugary foods, wholemeal foods, fruit and vegetables, bread or potatoes; or you may like to use the groups on page 16. Then count up the number of meals which contained these things.

Three ways of presenting your information are as:

Fractions
For example, if you looked at 10 meals, and perhaps 7 of them contained a fried food, then you would say that $7/10$ pupils chose meals containing fried foods.

Percentages
To work out a percentage you multiply the fraction by 100. For example $7/10 \times 100 = 70\%$ of pupils chose meals containing fried foods.

Bar Charts
You can draw a bar chart like the one on page 13. Put the number of meals up the side, and the foods you have looked at along the bottom.

Now write your conclusions. What have you found out? What do you think of the choices pupils make? Could they have chosen more wisely? How could they be helped to choose more wisely? Don't forget to look at the overall choices pupils make for their meals. Comment on the mixture of foods each pupil chooses.

If you studied packed meals as well as school meals, how did they compare?

Further work

1 This survey could be tried on different age groups, on boys and girls or on teachers, by different members of the class to see if there are any differences. How would you explain any differences? Remember you are only looking at very small numbers.

2 Write a short leaflet and illustrate it, to help pupils choose food wisely.

Shopping surveys

Here are some different types of surveys you might like to try.

Prices

Find out the price of these 10 foods in three different shops. If possible visit a supermarket, a small shop, and another shop. Find the price of the cheapest brand of each food.

Shops people use

Interview people in your local shopping area about the shops that they use and why they prefer them. Work out your questions before you start, for example:
1 Where do you do most food shopping?
2 Why do you like that shop best?
3 Which other shops do you use for shopping?
4 How do you travel to the shops?

When you write up your results you could note any differences between the preferences of:
a younger and older people,   b people with and without cars.
How do small local shops compare with supermarkets for popularity?

Discussion points

Do people really save money in a supermarket, or do they buy more food and eat more expensively because there is so much to choose from?

Write up your results and explain what you have found out.

Further work

Find or draw a map of your local area and show on it the location of small local shops, specialist shops, and supermarkets.

Find out the prices of well known brands of foods and compare these with the cheaper foods you have studied.

Can you remember what you ate?

Copy this table into your book or folder then write down everything that you ate yesterday, the day before, and one weekend day. If you find it difficult to remember, discuss it with a friend to help jog your memory. Thinking about what you did sometimes helps!

	Foods eaten		
	Yesterday	The day before	One weekend day
Breakfast or morning snack			
Midday meal			
Evening meal			
All other snacks and meals			

You can use the following groups of foods to analyse what you ate:

Group 1 Cereal foods and starchy vegetables
Group 2 Fruit and vegetables (include unsweetened fruit juices)
Group 3. Meat and alternatives
Group 4 Milk and milk products (e. g. cheese and yogurt)
Group 5 Sugar and sugary food and drinks
Group 6 Fats and oils

Underline all group 1 foods in blue, group 2 in yellow, group 3 in green, group 4 in brown, group 5 in black, and group 6 in red. You can also use the groups on p. 14. Many foods will need to be underlined more than once.

Questions

Sit in pairs or groups of three or four and discuss these questions before you write your answers.

1 Did you eat some fruit or vegetables at every meal including breakfast?
2 Which meals, eaten in your group, contained a lot of fibre?
3 Did any of you eat a lot of sweet or fatty foods?
4 How many reasons can you think of for not eating sweet and fatty foods?
5 How could you change your choice of food and cooking methods to eat less sweet and fatty foods?
6 Are there differences between weekday and weekend food?
7 How nutritious were the drinks you chose?
8 Think of five reasons why you need to eat plenty of fruit and vegetables, and other fibre-containing foods.

Your teacher might also ask you to report back to the class on your findings.

Further work

1 If you have access to a computer and a program which analyses diet you can obtain much more accurate information to help your discussions.

2 Carry out a survey to find out what are the most popular and the most unpopular foods. Different groups of people could be questioned by different members of your class, then you can compare your results. Are the most popular foods the ones which are best for you, for example fruit and vegetables or wholemeal foods? Draw a bar chart showing the popularity of different foods.

3 Carry out a snack survey. Find out which are the most popular snack foods and draw a bar chart to show your results.
You could also try to find out how many packets of crisps, sweets, and other snacks are bought by your class each week.
How much does this cost?
How could this money be better spent?
Watch and keep a record of television advertisements for snack foods.
How might these influence what we buy?

4 Find out which foods are eaten on special religious days and on festival days.

5 Write a paragraph on 'The foods people choose to eat'. Write another paragraph on 'The foods people should choose to eat' using ideas from your discussions. If you want to check any information about nutrition look it up in a school text book or a reference book.

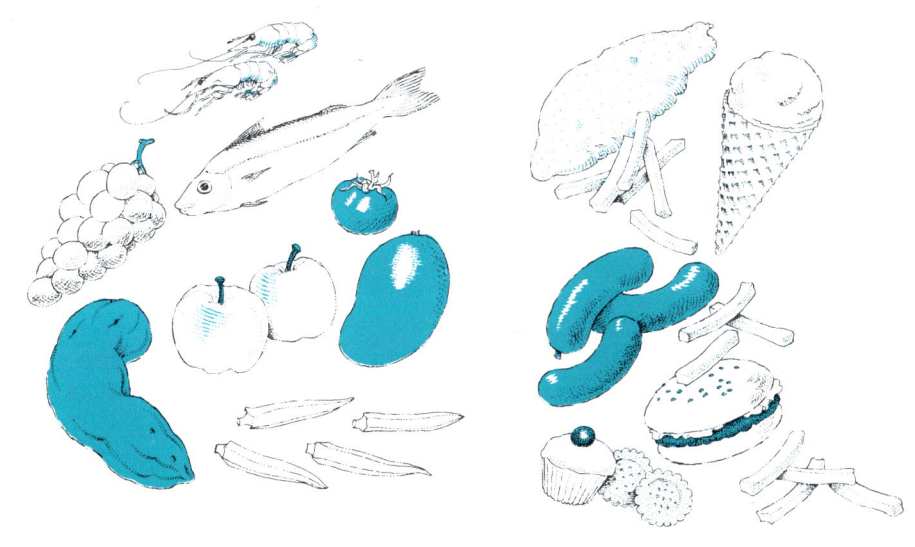

Some nutritious, and some not so nutritious foods

Cheese tasting

This works well in small groups of about four people.

> a plate
> 4 or more different cheeses, cut a piece of each cheese for everyone in your group to try
> cheese labels with prices

Copy out this results chart in your workbook.

Cheese tasting					
Name of cheese	**Texture** (e.g. crumbly, hard, soft)	**Appearance** and **colour**	**Taste** (e.g. strong, mild)	**Country of origin**	**Cost** per lb. or 500 g

Taste the cheeses one at a time and fill in the chart. You may wish to have a sip of water between tastings.

Questions

1 Which cheeses did you like best? Which was the most popular cheese in your group and in your class?
2 Has anyone tried new cheeses which they would like to try again?
3 Which were the cheapest and most expensive cheeses?
4 In the food industry any new food is tasted by a large number of people. Why do you think this is the case?

Cheese tasting

Further work

1 Carry out a simple survey in your class, amongst teachers or at home to find out which are the most popular cheeses. Draw a bar chart of your results. Try to decide why some cheeses are more or less popular than others, is it cost, advertising, convenience, uses or other reasons? Do adults and children make different choices?
2 Find out as much as you can about the making, selling, and cooking of cheese around the world.

Milk tasting

> samples of four or five different types of milk in jugs labelled only with numbers (about 50 ml per person), you could include goats' milk as well as different types of cows' milk
> a glass or beaker each
> microscope and microscope slides (if available)

1 Copy the results chart into your book or folder.

\multicolumn{5}{c	}{Milk tasting}
Sample number	Colour	Taste (e.g. sweet, watery, creamy)	Comments for example, did you like this milk?	Type of milk, packaging and cost (to be filled in later)

2 Try a little of each milk in turn and fill in the chart.
   Leave the 'Type of milk' column blank for the moment.
3 If possible look at small drops of the different milks under the microscope. Put a drop on a slide and cover with another slide.
4 When you have finished your tasting your teacher will tell you which milk is which so that you can complete your chart.

Questions

1 Which milks did you like best?
2 Which types of milk are the most popular in your class?
3 Which milks might be useful in cooking, even if they are not good to drink? Give reasons.
4 Was it important that you did not know which type of milk you were tasting? Give reasons.

Further work

1 List all the different types of milk that are sold in your local supermarket. Find out the cost of each one, and how long each one can be stored. Notice which ones have a 'cream line'.
2 What are the possible health risks of eating too many foods such as milk, cheese, butter, and animal fats?
3 There are lots of simple surveys that you can do related to milk. For example, you could find out which types of milk people buy, where they buy milk, and in what quantities.

Food labels and additives (1)

Food labels

Food labels give you a lot of information. You may find a date stamp which tells you when the food should be sold by and nutritional information which may tell you how much energy, fat, and fibre there is in a normal serving. The main thing to look for on food packets is the ingredients list. The higher up the list something comes the more there is of it in the food. Towards the bottom of the ingredients list is a list of food additives.

Food additives

Additives are often put into processed foods to keep them fresh or to 'improve' their colour, flavour or texture.

Modern food processing and the use of some additives enable us to eat a wide variety of foods all the year round. Without them our diets would be less varied and much food would be wasted. Some foods would also be more expensive.

Most additives probably do us no harm. Some, like the vitamins added to margarine, help us to have a balanced diet. Others such as preservatives help to prevent food poisoning. Some additives may be bad for us.

Many people are worried that we eat too many additives today. It is very difficult to know how safe food additives are. For example different countries allow, and ban, different additives. No one really knows the effects of eating additives for many years or the effects of eating lots of different additives. Perhaps one answer is to look more carefully at food labels so you know what you are eating. Make sure that you eat plenty of fresh foods such as fruit and vegetables too.

CEREAL INGREDIENTS
Wheat bran, sugar, salt, malt flavouring, niacin, vitamin B_6, riboflavin (B_2), thiamin (B_1), vitamin D_3.

Typical Nutritional Composition per 100 grammes	
Energy	249 kcal / 1055 kJ
Protein (Nx631)	15.1 g
Available Carbohydrate	44.9 g
Dietary Fibre	28.6 g
Vitamins:	
Niacin	16.0 mg
Vitamin B_6	1.8 mg
Riboflavin (B_2)	1.5 mg
Thiamin (B_1)	1.0 mg
Vitamin D_3	2.8 µg
Iron	9.0 mg

Instant Delight
CHOCOLATE FLAVOUR DESSERT MIX • ADD MILK
Ingredients: Sugar, Modified Starch, Gelling Agents (E339, E450a), Fat-reduced Cocoa, Lactose, Salt, Flavourings, Colours (E122, E102, E142).
Net Weight 62 g

Here are some common examples of additives.

Nutritional additives: these add nutrients.
Usually vitamins such as riboflavin, niacin, thiamin (B vitamins) or cholecalciferol (vitamin D). Minerals such as iron and calcium are added to some foods.

Improvers: these give food required texture.
Emulsifiers e.g. E322. Stabilisers e.g. lecithin, pectin, methyl cellulose. Thickeners e.g. modified starch. Humectants (to prevent food drying out) e.g. glycerine, sorbitol. Anti-caking agents (to stop food sticking together). Acids and acidity regulators.

Colourings: these add colour. (E100–E180)
These usually have a name and letter or number, such as E160A or E100. Natural colourings such as saffron (yellow) or annatto (in butter and cheese) may also be added to food.

Preservatives: these help food last longer. (E200–E290)
Sulphur dioxide, sorbic acid, nitrates, and nitrites are preservatives. Antioxidants delay the spoilage of fats, e.g. ascorbic acid (E300–E321).

Flavourings: these are added to food to change the taste. Find some examples.

Looking at additives

Collect together five or six packets or tins of food such as: soup, cake mix, ice cream, pies, stock cubes, breakfast cereal, and margarine.

Copy this table into your book or folder. Write in all the additives you can identify under these five headings. Use the summary above to help you.

Foods	Flavourings	Colourings	Preservatives	Nutritional additives	Improvers

Further work

1. Look at some other packets and tins of food that you have at home and list the food additives under the five headings.
2. How might you reduce the number and amount of food additives you eat?
3. What are the advantages (good things) and disadvantages (bad things) of food additives?
4. Organize a debate in your class about food additives.

Food labels and additives (2)

Looking at colouring in food

Colourings are added to make food look more attractive. They may be natural or made by manufacturers.

> different coloured smarties
> filter paper or coffee filter paper
> glass of water for moistening smarties
> dropper pipette or teaspoon

1 Moisten the smarties and touch them onto the filter paper. Label the different colours. What do you see?
2 Add drops of water slowly and carefully on top of the smarties. What happens?
When dry, the filter papers can be stuck into your workbook with your notes on the experiment. Try to explain your results. (This is a simple version of the chromatography that you might have tried in science.)

Questions

1 How do you think that the colouring for different smarties might be made?
2 Do you think that it is always necessary for food manufacturers to add colouring to food? Could you get used to canned peas which were grey, the colour they would be after canning without colouring?

Looking at flavouring

What differences can you find between fruit yogurt, fruit-flavoured yogurt, and home-made yogurt?

> 1 carton orange yogurt
> 1 carton orange flavoured yogurt
> 1 carton natural yogurt
> (keep all the cartons to compare the contents)
> (you can use another fruit if you wish)
>
> 1–2 teaspoons sugar
> 2 bowls
> 1 orange
> teaspoons

1. Peel and chop the orange finely.
2. Divide the natural yogurt into two bowls.
3. Add half the orange to half the yogurt.
4. Add the other half of the orange to the other half of the yogurt and also add the sugar.
   Taste a little of each of the four types of yogurt and then look at the cartons. Discuss the results with other members of your group. Write a summary of your findings.

Fruit drink comparison
Collect together as many different types of orange and orange-flavoured drink as you can find. These could include fresh, frozen, tinned, bottled or carton-packed orange juice as well as squash and orange drinks. Taste a little of each and check the labels, then write about your findings.

Crisp flavours
For this test you will need two or three flavours of crisps, three saucers and some volunteers to taste the crisps.

1. Put two crisps from one packet onto two saucers and label them with different letters or symbols.
2. Put a crisp from another packet onto a third saucer and label this too.
3. Ask your tasters to hold their noses and taste each crisp in turn to see if they can find the odd one out.
4. Repeat the test with further crisps and without holding noses. Discuss your results.
   Tests to spot the odd one out are called triangle tests and are often used by manufacturers when developing new food products.

Further work

1. Sugar is frequently added to food to 'improve' its flavour. Look at the labels of 10 or 20 different foods to see how many of them contain sugar. Include sauces, soups, and savoury foods as well as sweet ones. Remember the higher sugar is in the list of ingredients the more there is in the food compared to other things.
   (Sugar may also be listed as honey, molasses, sucrose, dextrose, fructose or glucose.)
2. Look at the ingredients' lists on different food packets at home and see how many food colourings and flavourings you can find. The information on page 21 might be helpful.

Can I trust the information?

You can obtain information about food and about the home from your experiments and from books and leaflets, but it is important to be critical.

Always ask yourself three questions.
1 Do I have all the information I need?
2 Is it correct?
3 Is it **biased** (one-sided)?

You can use the information you have got more easily when you have the answers to these questions.

Leaflets used in Home Economics

Many booklets and leaflets used in Home Economics are produced by food manufacturers. They are well presented and they are free or cheap. They include useful information *but* they may be biased as the manufacturers want you to use their product. You can be selective and use only the information you want.

Collect together four or five recipe booklets or leaflets produced by any food manufacturer. These should be available in your Home Economics room.

Discuss these questions then write out and complete the table below.

Name of the product and the firm who make it	How many times is the product mentioned in the leaflet?	Could another food be used instead of it?	Is there any other useful information in the leaflet?	Would you use the leaflet?	Give your reasons

Questions

1 What are your conclusions from this work?
2 What are the advantages (good things) of free recipe and information leaflets?
3 What are the disadvantages (bad things) of these leaflets?

Nutritional studies

These are very difficult to assess because they are so complicated and because people have such strong views about them.

Here are two extracts from two newspaper articles expressing different views about fat in the diet. Read them, then answer the questions.

Running to Fat

Doctor and medical writer James Le Fanu says we can relax—for most of us, meat, butter and cream are perfectly safe.

THE IDEA that eating less fat helps prevent heart disease has, by now, become a truism. What is lacking, however, is any real evidence that it is actually true. On the contrary, over the past 10 years the largest and most expensive medical experiment ever mounted has suggested that for the great majority of the population, eating fat makes no difference whatever.

FIGHTING OVER FAT

Annabel Ferriman, our Health Correspondent, on a medical controversy

All smoking, sedentary fatties are waiting for the definitive newspaper article proclaiming: 'Sloth, smoking and gluttony good for you — official.' Dr Le Fanu's recent article on fat consumption (8 July) served that purpose for readers partial to butter, cream cakes and full fat cheese. It was wonderful news, but is it true?

Medical experts have made the following criticisms of Dr Le Fanu's article:

- Part of the World Health Organisation trial, the Belgian section, showed that dietary change *was* useful. There was a significant reduction in both the incidence of coronary heart disease (CHD) and deaths from it, amongst the group who changed their fat intake.
- A high fat diet does not only increase the risks of CHD but also that of other disorders, such as high blood pressure, certain cancers and obesity.

Questions

1. Why is it so difficult to prove that eating certain foods when you are young will make you more or less likely to become ill when you are older?
2. Which is the main disease, mentioned in both articles, that some people believe is linked to eating a lot of fat?
3. What evidence does James Le Fanu give for saying that eating fat makes no difference to the health of most people?
4. What evidence do medical experts, mentioned in one of the articles, give for suggesting that a high-fat diet is a risk to good health?
5. What are your views?
6. Collect any articles you can find about food and nutrition to help you to make up your mind. Be careful to see who has written them.

You may also see advertisements, articles or booklets written by butter and margarine manufacturers. Why are these likely to be very different from each other? Look at the examples below and compare the information they give you.

Instead of butter...

Use margarines high in polyunsaturates.

...about health

Some people seem to feel that it maybe healthier to eat margarine than butter. Are they right?

No. Apart from the fact that margarine brands differ enormously in their composition, no medical research has shown a net benefit from changing over from animal fats. Whatever anyone says, the truth is that no improvement in life expectancy has been observed in trials designed to test this.

Section 2
Basic foods and mixtures

Plant cells

Here are some simple investigations to help you look at plant cells. Plant cells have cell walls which are important in cookery. We often cook vegetables to soften the cell walls. This makes the vegetables easier to eat.

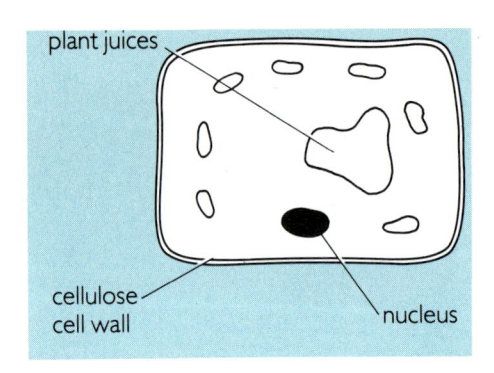

Investigation of carrot cells

| 2 carrots | a little salt | small saucepan |
| microscope | × 10 magnification lens | 4 microscope slides |

Test 1—To see how cooking softens cell walls
1. Put on a small saucepan of water with a little salt to boil.
2. Peel one of the carrots and slice it into rings.
3. Cook half the carrot rings for 8–10 minutes.
4. Drain the carrot rings and place them on a plate with the raw carrot rings.
5. Try to mash the two types of carrot with a fork. What happens?
6. Observe the carrots carefully. What differences in colour, texture, and taste can you see and feel?
7. Cut a very thin slice of raw carrot. Put it between two microscope slides. What can you see? Draw what you see.
8. Cut a very thin slice of cooked carrot. Put it between two microscope slides. What can you see? Draw what you see.

Test 2—To compare the effects of moist and dry heat on carrots
1. Take a few slices of raw carrot and cook them under the grill.
2. Put them onto the plate with the raw and boiled carrots and compare all three.

Questions

1. Which is the best way to soften plant cell walls, heat alone (as in grilling) or heat and water (as in boiling)? Why?
2. Why do you think that tomatoes can be successfully grilled?

Cooking a vegetable

> 1½ small potatoes (or other root vegetables such as sweet potato)
> 1 saucepan   a slotted spoon   watch or clock

1. Half fill the pan with water and put it on to boil.
2. Wash the 1½ potatoes.
3. Chop up the half potato into small cubes.
4. When the water boils make a note of the time and put the whole potato and the cubes into the pan.
5. After five minutes take out the whole potato and the potato cubes using the slotted spoon. *Do not* throw away the water.
6. Put the potato on a chopping board or plate.
7. Cut the whole potato in half and draw what you see in your notebook. Show the different layers.
8. Taste a little of this potato. What is it like?
9. Cut one of the potato cubes in half. Look at it, draw and taste it too.
10. Return all the potato to the pan and cook for a further 10 minutes.
11. Repeat the cutting, tasting, and drawing.
    You can use up any spare potato in a soup or a Spanish omelette.

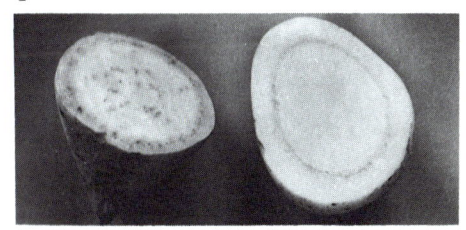

Partially cooked potatoes

Questions

1. What difference does chopping the potato have on cooking time?
2. There are two reasons why the heat can get into the potato cubes more quickly, what are they?

Further work

Look at small scrapings of raw and cooked potato under the microscope and draw what you see.

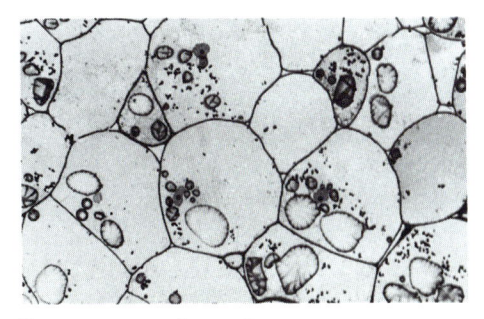

Raw potato under a microscope 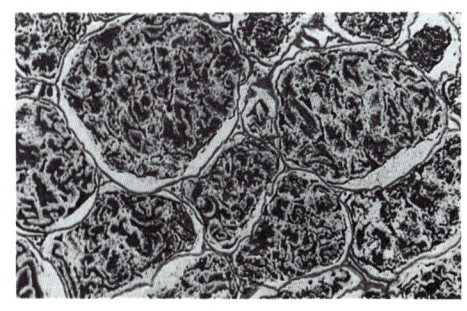   Cooked potato under a microscope

Tests with flour

Flour contains starch, dietary fibre, protein, B-vitamins, and minerals. In these two experiments you will be investigating the dietary fibre and gluten in flour. These are explained below and a test for starch is shown on page 63.

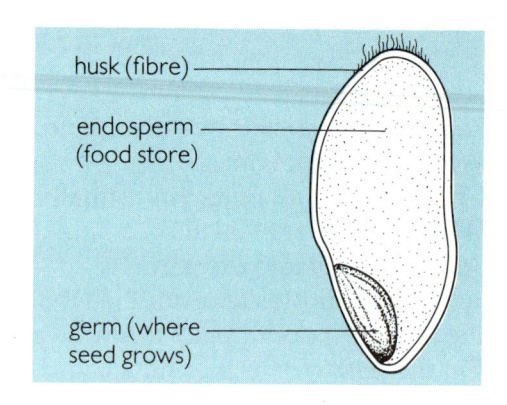

husk (fibre)
endosperm (food store)
germ (where seed grows)

Dietary fibre

Dietary fibre makes up the cell walls of plant foods such as wheat, other cereals, nuts, and fruit and vegetables. If you sieve wholemeal flour the **bran**, which contains most of the fibre, will remain in the sieve.

The amount of water needed to make foods such as bread and pastry from wholemeal flour and refined flour (with bran removed) is not the same.

Try this simple test to see the difference.

30 g (1 well-rounded tablespoon) wholemeal flour
30 g (1 well-rounded tablespoon) self-raising flour
each in a small basin or cup   dropper pipette

1 Add water one drop (or teaspoon) at a time to the wholemeal flour until it forms a soft (not runny) mixture. Count how many drops you use.
2 Do the same with the self-raising flour.

Keep these mixtures as they can be used for the gluten test.

Questions

1 Which absorbs most water?
2 Which has the most fibre?
3 Which recipe will need more water, white bread or wholemeal bread? Why?
4 How might increasing dietary fibre help to prevent constipation?

Further work

Find out more about the importance of fibre in our food.

Gluten tests

Gluten is formed from two proteins in flour. It is stretchy and helps bread to rise.

> the wholemeal flour mixture and the self-raising flour mixture from the investigation of dietary fibre
> 30 g (1 rounded tablespoon) strong plain flour
> 3 small squares of muslin or 'J' cloth (preferably different colours) all the same size—about 10 cm square
> 3 tie closures

1. Mix the strong plain flour with enough water to make a soft dough.
2. Put the mixture into the centre of the piece of cloth, and fasten the mixture into the cloth using a tie closure.
3. Run cold water over the dough and squeeze it gently to wash out the starch. Save a little of the washed out water, and test it for starch (page 63).
4. When the dough has been washed for about five minutes and there seems to be no more starch coming out, put this ball of gluten to one side.
5. Repeat with the self-raising flour and then with the wholemeal flour. Do not mix up the three samples.
6. Weigh each ball of gluten with the cloth.
7. Try to roll each ball of dough into a sausage, compare the stretchiness.
8. If you wish you can bake the three small balls of gluten on a baking tray in an oven at gas 7/220°C/425°F. The more protein there is, the larger the ball of gluten. If you are not careful in your washing out you may not have enough gluten to bake.

Write up the results of your experiment in your workbook.

Questions

1. In which mixture is the most sticky gluten left?
2. From which mixture was the most starch washed out?
3. The best bread is made with flour which contains a lot of gluten, so which flour would be the best for making bread?

Further work

1. Try tasting small cubes of white and wholemeal bread. Compare the taste, texture, chewiness, and number of chews needed to soften the bread. How do they compare? Which type of bread do you think is more filling?
2. Make a list of foods you eat which contain flour.
3. Find out more about the manufacture of flour and about the nutrients found in plain and wholemeal flour.

Heating starch and sugar

These quick experiments or demonstrations show the effect of dry and moist heat on starch and the effect of heat on sugar. Flour is mainly made up of starch, a type of carbohydrate.

> plain flour (also cornflour if you wish to add further variations)
> water
> sugar
> a frying pan
> wooden spoon
> 2 small basins or saucepan
> a microscope if possible—use the ×10 magnification lens unless you are able to make *very* thin samples on your microscope slide in which case you can use the ×40 lens
> microscope slides (and coverslips)

One person could try all three of these variations or they could be shared between three people. The second and third variations are explained in numbers 7 and 8 below.

Moist heat on starch—gelatinization

1. Mix ½ teaspoon of flour with 2 teaspoons of water in a small basin. Does it dissolve easily?
2. Put a little drop of this mixture on a microscope slide. Cover it with another slide or a cover slip, trying not to trap any air bubbles. Look at it under the microscope. Can you see the **granules**? Draw what you see.
3. Heat and stir the rest of the mixture in a pan. What happens? Notice any slight colour changes.
4. Take a little smear of this flour starch, which has now been **gelatinized**, and put it on a clean microscope slide. Cover with another microscope slide or cover slip.
5. Look at it under the microscope. Have the starch granules swollen and burst? Draw what you see. Heating in this way has allowed the starch granules to burst then absorb water, and thicken the mixture.
6. Wash and dry the pan.
7. You can repeat the experiment with the same ingredients but this time do not stir the mixture. Describe and explain what happens.
8. You may also wish to repeat the experiment with cornflour.

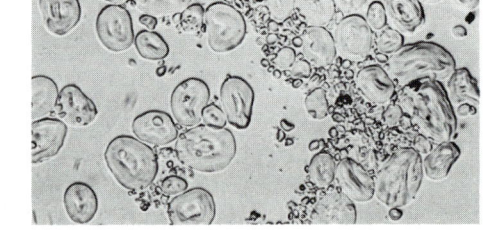

Starch granules under a microscope

Dry heat on starch—dextrinization

1. Gently heat ½ teaspoon dry flour in your pan. What happens to it? What is the smell like? Do not allow it to burn.
2. When it is slightly off white, add two teaspoons of water and stir well until it thickens. How does this compare with the last experiment?
3. If possible, take a little smear of this mixture and look at it under the microscope.

Next time you make toast, take note of the colour changes and taste a little of the browned surface. It is slightly sweeter than bread as the starch is changed into **dextrin** by the heat. Dextrin is easier to digest than starch which is why you can often manage to eat a piece of dry toast when you are too unwell to eat anything else.

Moist heat on sugar—caramelization

Put 1 tablespoon of sugar and 1 tablespoon of water into a clean pan and heat gently.

Observe it carefully and note the changes that take place. Have ready a small basin half full of cold water. Once the mixture starts to change colour, take out ¼ teaspoons at ½ minute intervals and put them into the water. You will see that the mixture gradually becomes harder. Do not burn the mixture. Take care not to allow the hot mixture to touch your skin. Write up your experiment and describe what happened. Explain how these results might be useful in cooking.

Questions

1. **Flour**
   a. Why is the flour cooked for a few minutes before adding the recipe liquid in a roux sauce?
   b. Why is it important to stir a sauce all the time while it is being made?
   c. Draw and label diagrams of raw and cooked starch grains in your workbook or folder, if you were able to observe them under the microscope.
2. **Sugar**
   What might you be making if you were boiling sugar?

Further work

1. Find out the method for making mixtures which are thickened by the gelatinization of starch such as gravy, custard, and white sauce. Try out one of these recipes and observe what happens very carefully.
2. Look up some recipes for sweets in a recipe book and find out about the stages in boiling sugar. What is the test for each stage?

Effect of heat on protein foods (1)

When most protein foods are heated, the protein **coagulates** (sets). If you could see what was happening to the protein molecules you would be able to see these changes in **some** protein foods:

uncooked

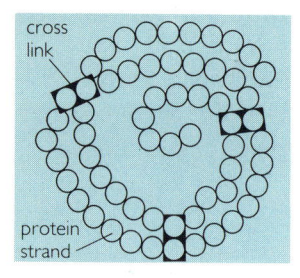

Coils of protein chains with cross-links.

cooked

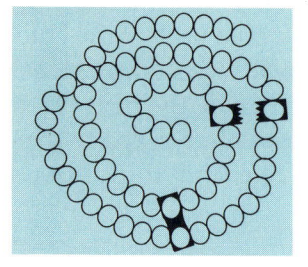

Links break, chains start to untwist and shrink. This may make the food harder.

over-cooked

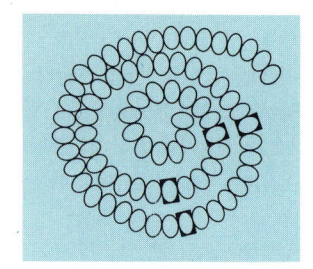

Protein molecules are packed more tightly together, making the food tough. Liquid may be squeezed out.

You can observe what happens to protein foods when they are heated.

Do the tests described in the next few pages when you are cooking protein foods. If you keep a careful record of all your results you will be able to compare the effects of heat on different types of protein foods.

Meat

Different cuts of meat need to be cooked in different ways. Some meat is much tougher than other meat because it comes from a part of the animal, such as the neck, which is used a lot. Meat from older animals is also tougher.

When meat is cooked correctly the tough **connective** tissue which holds the meat fibres together softens.

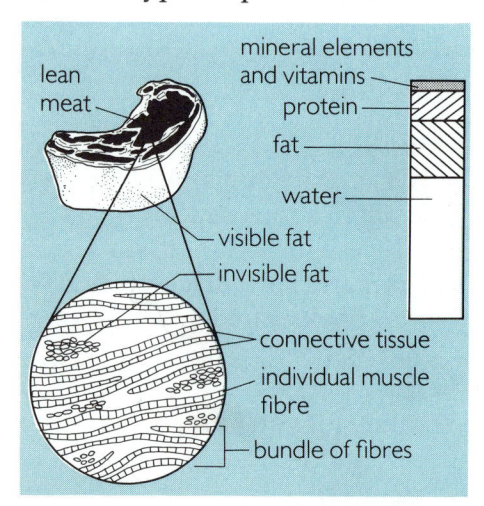

- 20 g shin of beef or other **tough** cut of meat
- 20 g rump steak or other **tender** cut of meat
- 2 small saucepans
- 2 pieces of foil about 7 cm square

1 Look at the two types of meat carefully.
2 Put them on a chopping board. Remember which is which. Cut each piece of meat in half. Which is easier to cut?
3 Put half of the rump steak into a small saucepan. Cover it with water.
4 Put half the shin into another saucepan and cover it with water.
5 Place the two uncooked pieces of meat onto two pieces of foil. Put them to one side and wash the chopping board.
6 When the pieces of meat have just come to the boil lift them out of the pan onto the chopping board and cut off and taste a little piece of each.
7 Return the meats to the correct pans.
8 Boil both pans gently for about 25 minutes. While they are cooking do the following:
9 Take the uncooked pieces of meat on the foil squares and grill them for three or four minutes. Cut off and taste a little of each, as before. How do they compare? Do not throw the foil away.
10 Continue grilling the meat for another five minutes, or until well done, then cut and taste them again. What do you notice? Compare and taste the meat juices too.
11 Cut and taste the meat which has been cooked in the water. How do they each compare with the grilled meats?
12 Taste a little of the cooking water. How does this compare with the juices from the grilled meat?

Copy out the results table in your workbook or folder and write in your results.

	When grilled	When stewed
Rump steak		
Shin of beef		

Explain what happened in your experiments. Which method is best for each type of meat?

Questions

1 Why is some meat more tender than other meat?
2 Why is rump steak so much more expensive than shin of beef?
3 Why are long, slow, moist methods of cooking often suggested for tough meat?
4 Why was it important to wash the chopping board after step 5 above?

Further work

1 Try these tests with non-muscular meat such as liver for comparison.
2 How can you adapt meat recipes to include less fat?

Effect of heat on protein foods (2)

Here are some more tests on protein foods for you to try. Remember that protein is usually hardened (coagulated) by heat.

Cheese

> 10 g cheese
> ¼ slice of bread
> a small piece of foil

1. Slice the cheese thinly.
2. Put half of the cheese on the bread, and half on the foil.
3. Heat both of these under the grill until golden brown.
4. Observe carefully what happens to the cheese. Taste it.
5. Write about what you have seen. What happens to the fat in both pieces of cheese?

Milk

> 50 ml milk   small saucepan
> teaspoon   cup or bowl
> fine mesh sieve

1. Heat the milk, watching carefully to see what happens.
2. When the milk boils, strain it into a cup or bowl through a sieve.
3. Taste the milk in the cup. How does it compare with unheated milk?
4. Taste a little of the substance in the sieve. This is coagulated milk protein. What does it taste like?
5. Write about your findings. Why doesn't the whole 50 ml of milk coagulate? How does milk differ from water when boiled?
   You can use up the milk in cooking or reheat it to make a drink.

Fish

> a small piece of any type of fresh fish (about 20 g)
> a small saucepan

1. Observe the fish carefully. Look at the way the flakes of fish are held together. Compare fish with meat. Meat has more **connective tissue** holding it together.
2. Put the fish into a small saucepan. Just cover with water.
3. Cook gently for three or four minutes until the flakes are starting to come apart when touched with a fork.
4. Put the fish on a plate or board. Use a fork to see how the flakes are held together. Taste a little of the fish.
5. Return the fish to the pan and cook for a further 5 mintues until the edge of the flakes look dry.
6. Observe and taste this fish.
7. Write up your results.

Can you boil an egg?

an egg for each person (work in groups of four)
a thermometer 0–110°C if available

Cook the egg according to the instructions beside the letter that you have been allocated. Use up your egg in a salad or other dish.

Cooking	Crack the shell gently when cooked	Cooling
A cook egg at 90°C (simmer it gently) for 10 minutes	yes	in cold water
B cook egg at 90°C (simmer it gently) for 10 minutes	no	leave in the air to cool
C cook the egg at 100°C (boil fiercely) for 10 minutes	yes	in cold water
D cook the egg at 100°C (boil fiercely) for 10 minutes	no	leave in the air to cool

When the eggs are quite cool, shell them and cut them in half.

Questions

1 Which eggs are easiest to shell?
2 Do any of the eggs have a greeny black ring round the yolk?
3 Were any eggs rather tough and rubbery? (Taste a tiny bit if you are unsure).
4 Which is the best way to cook and cool eggs?

True or false?

1 Coagulation is the hardening of protein food when it is heated.
2 Overcooked protein is soft and easy to digest.
3 When proteins are overcooked liquids such as water or fat may be squeezed out.
4 Tough meat should be cooked quickly using dry heat as this will help to soften the connective tissue.
5 Fish contains less connective tissue than meat so it can be cooked more quickly.

Mixtures in foods

When we are cooking we are often making mixtures of different foods. The type of mixture we want to make will affect the way that we make it. Some common types of mixture are:

A solution
Black instant coffee is a solution. In a **solution** one substance is completely **dissolved** in another. When the instant coffee is dissolved in hot water you cannot see the coffee particles even under a microscope.

An emulsion
Oil and vinegar salad dressing is an **emulsion**. In an emulsion tiny drops of one liquid are spread out in another liquid. You cannot see the droplets as they are very small, unless you use a microscope.

A suspension
A cup of 'real' coffee is a **suspension**. In a suspension very fine solid particles are spread out in a liquid, They will often settle to the bottom of the mixture if left to stand. Grounds settle out of a cup of 'real' coffee and are sometimes seen at the bottom of the cup.

Experiment to make stock

> 1 stock cube cut into four equal sized pieces
> 4 heat resistant glass tumblers or small measuring jugs
> cold and boiling water, take care!
> 4 labels A, B, C, and D
> 1 teaspoon

1 Put about 50 ml of cold water into two heat resistant glasses.
2 Put the same amount of boiling water into two other glasses.
3 (A) Add ¼ stock cube to the glass of cold water without crumbling.
  (B) Add ¼ stock cube to the glass of hot water without crumbling.
  (C) Crumble ¼ stock cube into the glass of cold water.
  (D) Crumble ¼ stock cube into the glass of hot water.
4 Leave the glasses to stand for five minutes. Make a note of what happens in each glass. Check to see if there is any stock cube at the bottom of the glass.
5 Stir each glass of stock once or twice.
6 Leave to stand for another five minutes then make a note of what happens. Write up your results so far.

Questions

1 Which is the most effective way of dissolving a stock cube? Why?
2 Is this mixture a solution, a suspension or a mixture of the two? How can you tell?

Emulsions in salad dressings

An emulsion is a special type of mixture where tiny droplets of one liquid, such as oil, spread throughout another liquid, such as vinegar. In cooking we often want to make stable emulsions which last well and do not separate out.

Emulsifying agents, such as egg, can help an emulsion to last longer and be more **stable**.

What makes an emulsion more stable?

> 4 test tubes labelled 1 to 4
> test tube rack
> 4 teaspoons oil
> 4 teaspoons vinegar
> pinch of mustard powder
> a ruler
> 2 teaspoons
> 1 teaspoon each egg yolk and egg white

1. Separate the yolk of the egg from the white.
2. Put one teaspoon of oil and one teaspoon of vinegar into each test tube.
3. Add nothing else to tube **1**, this is your **control**.
4. Add the following to the other tubes:
   tube **2**   1 teaspoon egg yolk
   tube **3**   1 teaspoon egg white
   tube **4**   pinch of mustard powder
5. Observe or measure the height of vinegar (bottom layer) and the total height of liquid in each tube.
6. Put your thumb over the control tube and invert it (turn it upside down) five times.
7. Observe the tube carefully just after mixing. Look at the size of the droplets. Measure the heights of the different layers if you want to.
8. Quickly repeat this method with the other three tubes.
9. Leave the tubes to stand for five minutes then observe them again.
10. With your thumb over the tubes shake them up really thoroughly. Observe each one just after mixing and after standing for five minutes. Don't forget to look at the size of the droplets as well as the heights of different layers.
11. Write up your results. What difference does thorough mixing make?

Further work

Many variations on this experiment are possible. You can investigate the effects of salt, pepper, whole egg or gelatine solution to see what happens.

Making dairy foods

You can easily make cheese, yogurt, and butter for yourself. This will help you to understand the manufacturing methods too.

Making butter

> 1 screw top jar with well-fitting lid
> cream from one pint of milk
> 1 glass or beaker
> a little salt (optional)

1 Put the cream into the jar. Screw on the top.
2 Shake the jar for about five minutes until creamy-yellow lumps of butter can be seen.
3 Pour off the liquid 'buttermilk' into a glass or beaker. Taste it if you wish.
4 Put the butter in a cool place. Add a little salt if you want to. Taste the butter.

Making Yogurt

> 1 vacuum flask or 1 clean glass beaker or other container
> a towel, muslin or 'J' cloth
> teaspoon
> 100 ml milk, preferably sterilized or 'long-life' (UHT) milk
> ½ small carton plain yogurt
> a thermometer is useful (but not essential for sterilized or UHT milk)

1 Warm the milk until it is just over blood heat, 43°C. (It will feel warm but not too hot to touch.)
(If you use unsterilized milk you will have to heat it to 70°C to kill the bacteria which would sour the milk, then let it cool.)
2 Add the yogurt and stir.
3 Put into the flask or beaker and cover.
4 If you are using the beaker leave on or near a radiator, or other warm place overnight.
5 By next day the bacteria in the yogurt will have turned the milk into yogurt too.
Keep some yogurt to make cheese and for the pH test shown on page 60.

Making cheese—method 1

> 4–5 tablespoons natural yogurt
> 1 small basin
> ½ clean 'J' cloth or similar cloth

1 Put the yogurt into the cloth.

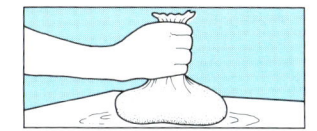

2 Gather up the cloth round the yogurt.

3 Put the cloth full of yogurt into the basin.

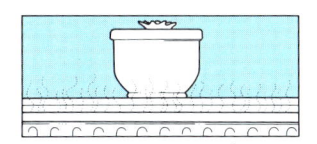

4 Leave overnight in a warm place.

5 The next day squeeze the cloth gently to remove some liquid.

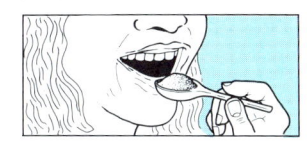

6 Taste the 'cream cheese' left in the cloth.

Making cheese—method 2

100 ml milk
½ teaspoon lemon juice
piece of muslin or 'J' cloth about 10–15 cm square
1 teaspoon rennet
1 saucepan
sieve

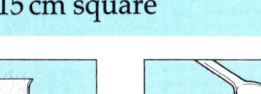

1 Warm the milk to blood heat (37°C). It should not feel hot or cold.

2 Add the lemon juice and rennet.

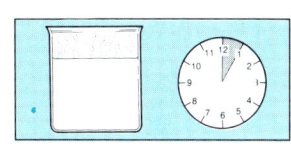

3 Leave for five minutes.

4 Strain through the cloth inside a sieve.

5 Gently squeeze out the watery whey.

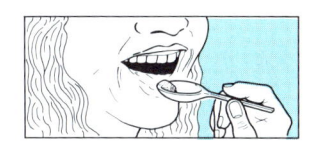

6 Taste a little of the cheesy curds left in the cloth.

This mixture does not keep well because of the way it has been made to speed up the setting.

Further work

See if you can find articles in the newspapers about the possible health risks of eating too many fats, particularly animal fats such as dairy foods. What is your view of any article that you find?

Section 3
Equipment, and experimental cookery

Choosing equipment

How should you choose the best equipment for cooking? The only way to be sure is to try the different pieces of equipment for yourself and see which ones work best. Cost must also influence your choice.

When you are making a simple dish such as cheese and potato pie, coleslaw or a salad, or another recipe which includes peeling, slicing, and grating, try this simple experiment.

> a range of peelers, graters, knives, and other equipment available in your Home Economics room which could be used for peeling, slicing, and grating
> a food processor makes a good comparison if available

Share out the pieces of equipment between members of the class.

Time your work carefully.
Notice whether they are easy or difficult to use.
Notice and weigh the amount of waste produced.
Check to see how easy and quick the equipment is to clean.

Lay out your results in a table as shown on the next page. Discuss the work with other members of your group or class.

Equipment	Time taken	How easy to use	Amount of waste	Ease of washing	Comment	Cost

For **peeling** compare:
  a serrated knife
  a vegetable (paring) knife
  a vegetable peeler

For **slicing and chopping** compare:
  a serrated knife
  a vegetable (paring) knife
  a French cook's knife
  an autochop
  a food processor (if available)

For **grating** compare:
  a mouli-grater
  a tall grater
  an autochop
  a food processor (if available)

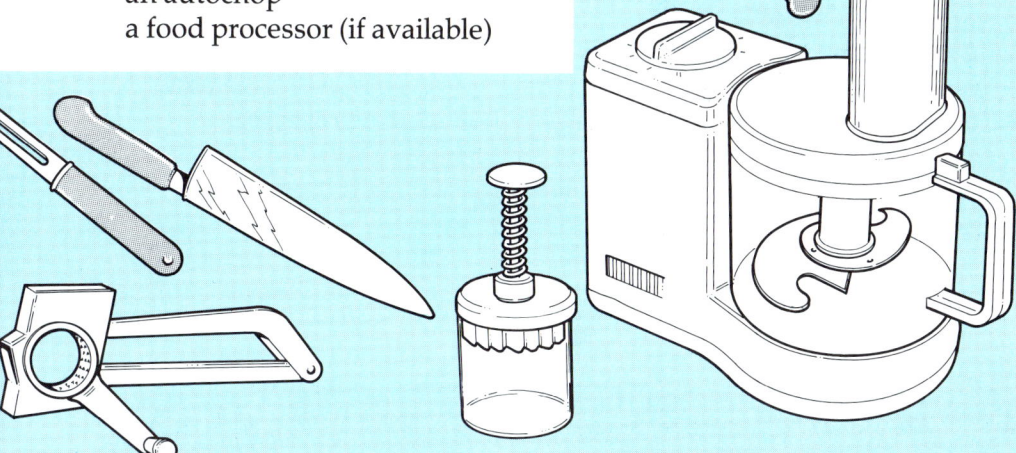

Results and conclusions

1 When you have finished, fill in the chart in your workbook using your own and other people's results.
2 Write your conclusions. Which are the best and worst pieces of equipment. Give reasons.

Further work

1 Find out the cost of the equipment used in your experiment.
2 Repeat this experiment using equipment available at home.
3 Work out similar experiments using other recipes and other equipment.

Evaluating large equipment

Here are tests to compare gas, electric, and microwave cookers, the effects of using different oven shelves and the effect of using a pan lid.

Experiment to compare different cookers

> a gas cooker set at mark 7
> an electric cooker pre-heated to 220°C/425°F
> a microwave cooker
> 3 baking trays
>
> **Ingredients for scones:**
> 200 g wholemeal self-raising flour
> 25 g margarine
> 4–5 tablespoon milk
> 1 tablespoon sugar

1 Make up one recipe of scone mixture. Rub the fat into the flour, then add the sugar, then the milk. Roll the dough and cut out the scones.
2 Put a third of the scones onto each baking tray and cook them as follows:
   a Cook a third of your scones on the top shelf of a gas oven at mark 7.
   b Cook a third of your scones on the top shelf of an electric oven at 220°C/425°F.
   c Cook a third of your scones in a microwave cooker following the manufacturer's instructions.

When they are cooked, compare them for time taken, colour, flavour, and texture. Say which you like best and least, and give reasons.

Scones cooked in:

| a microwave oven | a gas oven | an electric oven |

Further work

You can make these comparisons with any other foods that you bake.

Experiment to compare the temperatures of different oven shelves

½ slice of bread for each oven shelf in the three cookers you are comparing
1 gas and 2 electric cookers

1 Turn one of the electric cookers on at 200°C and let it come up to the correct temperature.
2 Turn on the other two cookers (gas mark 6/200°C). Put a ½ slice of bread on each shelf of each of the 3 cookers.
3 Leave the cookers on for 10–15 minutes then remove the bread to compare your results.

Bread cooked in:

| an electric oven | a preheated electric oven | a gas oven |

Discuss and write up the results. What will you need to remember when cooking in these ovens in the future?

Further work

Try this experiment when you are baking bread, scones or cakes and notice the differences.

Experiment to check the effect of using a pan lid

1 Use two pans which are the same size and made of the same material. Use equal-sized hot plates or burners.
2 Put 200 ml of water into each pan.
3 Put a lid on one pan. Put both pans on the cooker and carefully check the time taken for each to come to the boil.
4 Explain your results and anything else you observe.
5 You can also compare the time taken to boil the same quantity of water in a kettle, but take care to cover the element.

Further work

Find copies of the magazine 'Which?' in your Home Economics room or library. Look at their comparisons of any piece of kitchen equipment and write about what they have found and what you think about the comparisons made.

Whisking egg whites

A whisked egg white is a **foam**. Bubbles of air are mixed into, and trapped by, the egg white. The way that the egg is whisked affects the amount of air that can be held by the egg white.

The first experiment investigates the effects of using different whisks. In the second experiment sugar is added to egg whites in different ways.

Use up the egg white in an appropriate recipe.

Experiment 1—Investigation of the efficiency of different whisks

> as many different whisks and mixers as possible
> a measuring jug or bowl of the same type for each person
> 1 size 3 egg for each person
> clock or watch

1 Separate the egg yolk from the white.
2 Put the egg white into a measuring jug, unless you are using a mixer which needs a larger bowl.
3 Make a note of the time, and whisk your egg until it stands in stiff peaks and can be turned upside down without falling out of the jug or bowl. Again note the time and work out how long it has taken.
4 Carefully measure the volume of the egg white in millilitres.
5 Clean your whisk. Was it easy?
6 Copy and complete the results chart, then use up your egg in an appropriate recipe.

Type of whisk	Time to whisk	Volume of egg	Ease of use	Ease of cleaning	Your comments on the results

7 Write your conclusions.

Questions

1 Which whisk takes the shortest time to whisk the egg white?
2 Which whisk produces the largest volume of egg white?
3 Which whisks are the easiest to use and clean?
4 Which would you prefer to use and why?
5 If one person whisked all the eggs how might the results differ?
6 What are the advantages and disadvantages of sharing the work?

Experiment 2—Adding sugar to meringue

> a whisk (all must be the same type)
> a measuring jug or bowl (all should be the same type and size)
> 1 egg (size 3)
> 1 tablespoon caster sugar

You will be allocated a letter. Follow the recipe for this letter.

A	Whisk the egg white until stiff. Whisk in the sugar lightly.
B	Whisk the egg white until stiff. Lightly fold in the sugar with a tablespoon using a figure of eight movement.
C	Whisk the egg white until stiff. Whisk in half of the sugar. Fold in half of the sugar using a tablespoon.
D	Put the sugar and egg white into the jug and whisk them together.
E	Whisk the egg white with some egg yolk. Whisk in the sugar lightly.

Perfect meringues

When you have finished, measure the volume of the finished egg and sugar.

Make a list of the methods used and the volumes produced. Put the mixtures on separate baking trays.

Bake these meringues at gas mark 5/180°C for 15 minutes and compare the finished results.

Questions

1 Which method of adding sugar do you think is the best?
2 Which methods do not work well?

Further work

1 Find out the costs of different whisks and mixers. Which do you think are the best value for money?

2 There are many possible variations on these experiments. For example you could investigate the effect of using granulated sugar, or of whisking the egg in a greasy bowl. You could also compare the effect of using different mixing bowls too.

Cooking eggs

When you cook an egg it becomes solid. This is called **coagulation**. Experiment 1 is a comparison of the effects of heat on whole egg, yolk, and white. Experiment 2 investigates the cooking of egg custards.

Experiment 1—What happens when eggs are heated?

> 1 egg
> 3–4 test tubes
> 2 clean cups or bowls
> 3 clean teaspoons
> a little milk (if required)
> 1 heat-proof glass beaker
> 1 saucepan or 1 gauze
> watch or clock

1 Separate the egg white from the yolk.
2 Spoon the egg into the three test tubes so that you have yolk in one, white in the second and a mixture in the third.
3 If you have any egg left you can put it into a fourth test tube with a little milk and compare the result.
4 Put the tubes into a beaker half full of cold water.
5 Heat the beaker on the cooker on top of the gauze or in a pan of water. Make a note of your starting time.
6 Record the time taken for each of the tubes:
  a to start coagulation (streaks form)
  b to complete coagulation (when the mixture is firm)

Questions

1 Exactly what happens when you heat **a** egg white **b** egg yolk **c** whole egg? Explain the stages the egg goes through.
2 Explain the word coagulation. See p 32 for more information.

Experiment 2—Which are the best ways of cooking egg custards?

When eggs are mixed with milk or other liquids they can still coagulate when heated.

> 6 small oven-proof dishes or foil dishes (All should be the same size if possible.)
> 50 g shortcrust pastry (This should be used to line two of the dishes.)
> 2 ovens, one at gas 4/180°C/350°F, the other at gas 8/230°C/450°F
> 2 sandwich cake tins half full of water (these are the water baths)
> 2 baking trays   300 ml milk
> 3 eggs   1 tablespoon sugar

1. Mix the egg, milk, and sugar in a bowl. This is the custard mixture.
2. Divide the mixture equally between the 6 dishes. On each baking tray put the following:

Gas mark 8 or Gas mark 4

water bath with one dish of custard mixture

pastry lined dish with custard mixture

dish of custard mixture

3. Put one tray on the top shelf of the hot oven, and the other tray on the top shelf of the warm oven.
4. Cook for 15 minutes then look at and taste the custards.
    a. Turn each one out onto a clean plate.
    b. Measure the depth with a skewer.
    c. Cut it in half to see whether it has **curdled**.
    d. Taste a little of each custard.
   As the custards in the warm oven need a little longer to cook, test the custards from the hot oven first.
   Fill in the results chart and discuss your results.

Curdled egg custard

Method	Temperature	Was it curdled?	Appearance	Taste	Your comments on the results

Questions

1. Which are the best ways to cook an egg custard? Why?
2. What happens when you overcook an egg custard? Why?

Further work

You can make custards with egg yolk and white alone to see what happens. List some dishes made with **coagulated** eggs.

Making cakes

There are two different experiments outlined below. The first is an investigation of the effects of different ingredients, and the second investigates the effects of different mixing and cooking methods.

To investigate the effects of different ingredients in cakes

Basic cake recipe
50 g SR flour preferably wholemeal
50 g caster sugar
50 g packet margarine
½ level tsp baking powder
1 egg (size 3)

9 paper cake cases
a label for each cake mixture

Cake mixtures	Variation
A control	basic cake recipe
B extra baking powder	1 heaped tsp baking powder
C extra sugar	100 g caster sugar
D no baking powder	no baking powder
E granulated sugar	50 g granulated sugar
F tub margarine	50 g tub margarine (polyunsaturated)
G reduced fat	30 g margarine

Each person or pair should make one of the cake mixtures.
Everyone must use the same method for this experiment.

Method

1. Set the oven at Gas 5/190°C/375°F.
2. Mix all ingredients together for 3 minutes.
3. Put into 9 paper cases.
4. Place on a baking tray labelled with the letter of your experiment.
5. Bake for 12–15 minutes.

To investigate the effects of different methods of mixing and cooking cakes

Everyone must use the same recipe in this experiment.

Basic cake recipe (see above)
9 paper cases for each cake mixture

Cake-making methods		
H **Use of microwave cooker** Mix all ingredients for 3 minutes. Put the cakes into double paper cases. Follow the manufacturer's instructions for cooking time.	**I** **Use of electric mixer** Mix all ingredients using an electric hand or table mixer. Note the time taken. Bake at gas 5/190°C/375°F for 12–15 minutes.	**J** **Shorter mixing** Mix all ingredients for 30 seconds only. Bake at gas 5/190°C/375°F for 12–15 minutes.
K **Longer mixing** Mix all ingredients for 10 minutes. Bake at gas 5/190°C/375°F for 12–15 minutes.	**L** **Oven higher** Mix all ingredients for 3 minutes then bake at gas 7/220°C/425°F.	**M** **Oven lower** Mix all ingredients for 3 minutes then bake at gas 1/140°C/275°F.

While the cakes are cooking, wash up and draw the results chart in your workbook.

Results of cakes experiments

Method used (A–M)	Size and shape	Appearance of both top and cut surfaces	Taste	Texture	Your comments on this result

When cooked put the cakes on a cooling tray.
For testing you will need to cut the cakes in half. It is more accurate to measure the size of the cakes than to guess their size. Use a ruler.
Observe and taste a little of the cake.
Fill in your section of the results chart.
Write out the complete chart into your workbook using everyone's results. Write up your conclusions explaining what to do and what not to do when making cakes.

Questions

1 Discuss the effects of all the variations in the recipe.
2 What are the best ways of making all-in-one cakes?
3 Explain why it is important not to eat too many cakes.
4 Compare the cost of these cakes with shop-bought cakes.
5 Work out and try further variations on this experiment.

⍭ Pastry making

Pastry can be made with a number of different ingredients. Here are some experiments to help you choose which way to make short crust pastry.

Each person or pair in the class will be making pastry in a different way. Use the variations shown on the results chart or add your own. Use your pastry to make savoury tartlets or jam tarts.

> ingredients and equipment for pastry making, including those listed on the table of results
> labels
> filling for tartlets—e.g. milk, egg and grated cheese or jam
> bun tin

1 Set the oven at gas 6/200°C/400°F.
2 Make up the pastry using one of the 10 variations in the table opposite using:
   in methods **1–6**   50 g plain flour
   fat as shown in the table opposite
   3 teaspoons of water (except method **6**)
   in methods **7–9**   flour as shown in the table opposite
   25 g block margarine
   3 teaspoons of water
   Rub the fat into the flour until it is like breadcrumbs. Then add the water. In method **10** follow the directions on the packet.
3 While your pastry is cooking, wash up and write out your results chart.
4 When the pastry is cooked, observe and taste it. Fill in your section on the summary chart. Complete your chart using the results of the other people in your class.

Conclusions

Write up your conclusions from your experiment. Say which are the good and bad ways to make pastry. Is one method better than all the others?

Questions

1 Are these results completely reliable?
2 How could the results of this type of experiment be made more accurate?
3 Compare your results with others in your class.

Pastry results chart				
Fat to be used or **variation**	**Colour and appearance**	**Texture** (Is it tough, crumbly, crisp, hard for example?)	**Taste**	**Comments**
1 use 25 g hard (block) margarine (control recipe)				
2 use 25 g butter				
3 use 25 g soft (tub) margarine				
4 use 25 g lard				
5 use 12½ g lard and 12½ g block margarine				
6 use 6 tsp water and 25 g block margarine				
7 use SR flour and 25 g block margarine				
8 use wholemeal flour and block margarine				
9 use 25 g wholemeal and 25 g plain flour				
10 use packet pastry mix				

Further work

1 Work out some other variations and try them. Try making pastry with a little less fat, for example.
2 How do home-made pastries compare for cost, time, and taste with frozen pastry?
3 Try making pastry with a little more fibre.
4 Compare the pastries for good storage.

What does yeast need to grow?

The demonstration and the experiment that follows it help to show what yeast needs to grow. When yeast grows it produces a gas called **carbon dioxide**. We can see if carbon dioxide has been made by collecting it in a balloon or bubbling it through lime water. Lime water goes cloudy when it is in contact with carbon dioxide. In cooking, carbon dioxide helps to make food rise.

Demonstration of the effect of food, water, and warmth on yeast

1 Set up the apparatus as shown in the diagrams. Your teacher may do this for you.

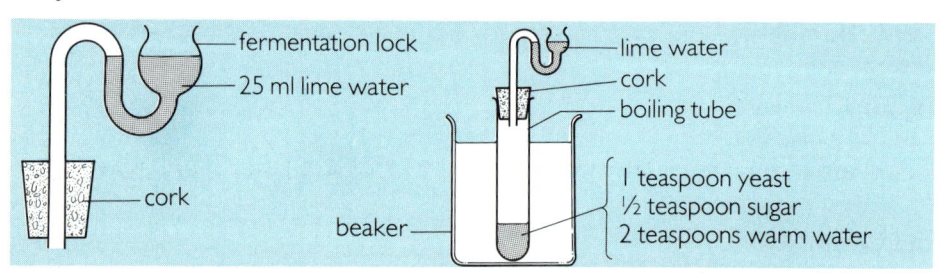

- fermentation lock
- 25 ml lime water
- cork
- lime water
- cork
- boiling tube
- beaker
- 1 teaspoon yeast
- ½ teaspoon sugar
- 2 teaspoons warm water

2 Leave to stand for about 10 minutes. What has happened?
3 Draw the diagrams of the apparatus in your workbook or folder. Write up the experiment and explain what has happened.

Experiment to compare the effects of different conditions on the growth of yeast

To look at the effects of food, water, and warmth, set up tubes A–D. If you also want to see what happens when yeast is mixed with boiling water set up tube E too.

5 beakers	kettle
5 balloons	5 test tubes
30 g fresh yeast	15 g caster sugar
a few ice cubes	

Set up the five test tubes as described in the table opposite. Tube A is described in detail below.

Tube A
1 tsp yeast
2 tsp warm water
½ tsp sugar

Put a balloon onto the tube.

Place it in a beaker half full of warm water.

This tube has food, water, and warmth. This is your **control**.

Tube	Put a balloon onto the tube	Place in a beaker ½ full warm water
A control	yes	yes
B no sugar	yes	yes
C no water	yes	yes
D no heat	yes	ice cold water
E boiling water	yes	boiling water

Leave these tubes for about 15 minutes but look at them every five minutes to see if the yeast is bubbling and if the balloon has expanded.

When you have looked at the tubes and made a note of the results, you can put tube D into a beaker of warm water. The yeast should then start to produce carbon dioxide. Why is this?

Does the yeast die at low temperatures?

Results

Copy the results chart into your workbook or folder and fill in the results.

	Yeast experiments				
Method	A	B	C	D	E
Did the yeast produce carbon dioxide?					

Describe each method used. What are your conclusions?

Questions

1 What slows the growth of yeast?
2 What kills yeast?
3 Under what conditions does yeast grow best?
   Remember these things when making bread.

Further work

You can try a number of different variations on this experiment. Try adding salt instead of sugar and try adding flour instead of sugar. Work out your own variations too.

Preserving apples

Foods may be preserved so that they can be kept for longer without spoiling. This experiment gives you a chance to see the effects of different ways of preserving apples or other fruit. Keep your foods for about three weeks before tasting and comparing the results.

Leave one small cooking apple in a cool place so that you can compare it with the others after three weeks.

Method A: Frozen apple (blanched)

> 1 cooking apple
> 1 tablespoon lemon juice
> 1 saucepan
> bowl or basin
> colander, sieve or blanching basket

1 Put on a pan of water to boil.
2 Peel, core, and slice the apple. Put the slices into a colander or sieve or blanching basket which is resting in a basin of cold water and lemon juice.
3 Put the apple slices in the boiling water for two minutes (this is called **blanching** the fruit). It destroys the **enzymes**. These are substances found in food which if not destroyed, would change and discolour the food.
4 Strain off the boiling water into the sink.
5 Plunge the apple slices into ice cold water for one minute.
6 Drain the apple slices well and let them cool.
7 Wrap, label, and freeze the apple slices.

Method B: Frozen apple (unblanched)

> 1 cooking apple
> a little lemon juice

1 Peel, core, and slice the cooking apple. Sprinkle with lemon juice.
2 Wrap the slices in cling film or place in a plastic bag.
3 Label and freeze the apple.

Method C: Frozen apple (unblanched, no lemon)

> 1 cooking apple

1 Peel, core, and slice the apple.
2 Wrap the slices in cling film.
3 Label and freeze.

Method D: Apple jam

> 1 cooking apple
> equal weight of sugar
> 2–3 tbs. water
> jam jar and cover

1 Peel and chop the apple.
2 Cook the apple gently with water until it is soft.
3 Add the sugar and boil until it is set. This will not take long.
4 Test it by putting ½ teaspoon jam onto a cold saucer or plate. When the jam has cooled it should wrinkle when touched.

After three weeks look at your samples and taste them. Compare them with the control—the apple that has been kept in a cool place during this time. Copy out this chart into your workbook and fill it in.

	Preservation		
Food and method of preservation	Changes in colour and appearance	Changes in texture	Your comments on this method

Method for vegetable preservation

If you wish to carry out this experiment with vegetables such as sprouts or green beans you can use some of the methods above with these variations.

A—leave out the lemon juice, blanch for 3 minutes
B—leave out this variation
C—as above
D—try a pickle recipe instead
E—alternate layers of vegetable with thick layers of salt in a clean jam jar

Cook samples **A**, **C** and **E** before tasting. Rinse sample **E** well before cooking.

Questions

1 What are the best methods of preservation?
2 Why are some methods of preservation more popular than others?

Further work

1 Find out whether it is always necessary to blanch fruit and vegetables. Look at a recipe book or freezer book to find this information.
2 If you wanted to blanch larger quantities of food, what method would you use? Again use a recipe or freezer book.
3 Find out about commercial methods of preserving food including drying, accelerated freeze drying, canning, and quick freezing. Your teacher may give you information on these methods. Preservation is also a good topic for a project.
4 Try making jam in a microwave cooker and compare your results.

Convenience foods

'Convenience foods' are foods that have been partially prepared by the manufacturer to shorten the cooking time at home.

You can carry out this experiment on any food which can both be home-made and bought in a convenience form: for example, a packet, tinned or frozen made-up food such as shepherd's pie or a packet cake mix are good choices.

You can either make both foods yourself or pair up with someone else; one of you can make the food the traditional way and the other one can make up the convenience food. Record and compare your results very carefully, to decide which is best. Make a note of all your comparisons as you go along. Note time taken very carefully.

Here are some suggestions for a results chart. You can add extra columns if you wish, or change it.

Comparison of convenience and home-made food		
	Convenience food	Home-made food
How long did it take to make?		
How easy was it to make?		
How long did it take to cook?		
What ingredients were needed?		
What was the total cost?		
How much washing up?		
What was the size and weight of the food?		
What was the taste like?		
What was the texture like?		
What did it look like?		
Your comments on the result		

Write up your experiment and give your conclusions. Say which food is best value and which gives the best results. Which do you prefer and why? If other people in the class have made different foods find out about their results too.

Comparing convenience methods

For some foods such as pizzas there are several quick and convenient methods of making them. It is useful to know how much time and money, if any, they save. Here are some suggestions for recipes and convenience foods that you could compare.

1 Wholemeal yeast-based pizza—traditional method.
2 Wholemeal scone-based pizza—a quick method.
3 Wholemeal frying-pan pizza.
4 Wholemeal packet mix pizza (follow instructions on packet).
5 Ready-made wholemeal pizza from supermarket or Health Food shop.

Use the results chart on the previous page to record your results. Add a column for each type of pizza made.

For each pizza use the same topping, for example:

> 50 g cheese, grated
> ½ onion, chopped very finely
> ½ tsp basil or mixed herbs
> ½ small tin tomatoes, drained and mashed with a fork

You will be able to find recipes for the bases in most recipe books or your teacher will supply you with recipes.

Questions

1 Which recipe or method or convenience food did you prefer? Give reasons.
2 Which do you think offers the best value for money?
3 How easy and convenient are these convenience foods and quick methods?

Further work

1 What are the advantages (good things) and disadvantages (bad things) of convenience foods?
2 Write about the convenience foods that you use and how you find them useful.
3 Do you think it is important to learn how to prepare and cook foods by traditional home-made methods? Why?
4 Were your classmates able to 'spot' the difference between home-made and convenience pizza?
5 Visit the school canteen and find out what convenience foods the staff there use. Do they use *any* traditional home-made methods?

Section 4
Simple tests with food

Testing food for acidity

It is often useful in cooking to know how acid a food is. Acid foods taste sour. If food is very **acid** it may curdle milk, cream or egg mixtures. It can also damage your teeth. The opposite of acid is **alkaline**.

Alkaline mixtures, such as sodium bicarbonate in cake making, can give food a horrible taste unless mixed with a strong flavour such as ginger.

If you want to test accurately the acidity of a food, you can test it with **universal indicator** paper. Universal indicator paper changes colour according to the acidity of the food it touches. The full range of pH (or acidity) values is from 1–14.

← acids — neutral — alkalis →
red · orange · yellow · yellowish-green · green · greenish-blue · blue · violet
1 2 3 4 5 6 7 8 9 10 11 12 13 14

Testing food for acidity using indicator paper

banana	marrow	orange juice
salt	bicarbonate of soda	any fizzy drink
lemon juice	sugar	baking powder
orange squash		
universal indicator paper and colour chart		
saucers or testing tiles		
clean teaspoons		

Solid foods should be dissolved in a little water before testing.
1 Draw a results chart for your experiment.

Food	pH (acid foods have a lower pH value)

Include the results of other people in the class if they tested different foods.
2 Put a small sample of food onto a clean dry saucer or testing tile.
3 If the food is not already a liquid then liquidize it or crush it with a clean

spoon, add one teaspoonful of water, then mix.
4 Using dry hands dip a strip of indicator paper into the food. Look at the colour chart and write the pH of the tested food on your results chart.
5 Repeat the experiment for the other foods. If you use the same saucer, tile or teaspoon again make sure that you wash and dry it carefully first.

Throw your samples away after doing this test. The chemicals in universal indicator paper are not edible.

Making red cabbage indicator

You can do this test at home or in school—you need no chemicals and it is easy and fun. You cannot measure pH by this method.

> 50 g red cabbage   grater
> tablespoon   saucers for testing
> 2 bowls   teaspoon
> foods for testing including lemon juice and bicarbonate of soda.

An interesting comparison of raising agents can be made by testing baking powder and cream of tartar as well as bicarbonate of soda.

1 Grate the cabbage into a bowl.
2 Add enough cold water to just cover the cabbage.
3 Let it stand until the water is purple (about five minutes).
4 Strain the liquid into a bowl or measuring jug. This is your **indicator**.
5 Put 1 tablespoon of indicator liquid on a clean saucer.
6 Add 1 teaspoon of lemon juice. What happens? This is your result for an **acid** food.
7 Put 1 tablespoon of indicator liquid on a clean saucer and test it with ½ teaspoon bicarbonate of soda liquid. What happens? This is your result for an **alkaline** food.
8 Now you can test other foods if you wish.

Make a table of your results. You can use up the cabbage in a salad.

Questions

1 Which is the most accurate, indicator paper or red cabbage indicator?
2 List all the foods you have tested in order of acidity. Start with the *most* acid food (lowest pH) and end with the *least* acid food (highest pH).
3 Acid foods are used a great deal in cookery. Here are three uses and questions. You can test the pH of these foods to back up your answers.
   a Acid helps to tenderize meat. Why are tomatoes used in casseroles?
   b Jam made with acid fruits sets more easily. Find out from a recipe book which fruits are acid.
   c Acid foods protect vitamin C. Which acid foods could you put in a salad dressing to keep the vitamin C in the salad ingredients?

Food tests on yogurt and milk

Testing yogurt and milk for acidity

It is interesting to compare the acidity (or pH) of milk, natural yogurt, fruit yogurt, and flavoured yogurt.

As you saw on page 58, universal indicator paper can be used to test the pH of food. The more acid the food, the *lower* its pH value will be.

> 5 strips of universal indicator paper and a colour scale
> 2 teaspoons each of: milk
>   natural yogurt
>   fruit and/or flavoured yogurt
> clean container for each food (e.g. saucer or beaker)

1. Place a sample of each food into a separate container.
2. Test each food with indicator paper. Make a note of your results.
3. Write up your results. Make a list of the foods tested in order of pH with the most acid (lowest pH) first.

Questions

1. What is the pH of milk?
2. What is the pH of yogurt?
3. What have the bacteria in the yogurt done to the milk while changing it into yogurt?
4. Does adding sugar and flavouring to yogurt make it less acid?

Throw your samples away after doing this test. The chemicals in universal indicator paper are not edible.

Testing milk for freshness

This test should be carried out in an area away from food preparation. This test depends upon the fact that a chemical called **resazurin** turns from blue to pink then to colourless as the amount of oxygen in a solution goes down. The test can be set up quickly, perhaps at the beginning of a lesson, and the test tubes left and examined after 30 and 60 minutes. Bacteria use up oxygen as they grow. If there are many bacteria they will use up a lot of oxygen and the colour will change quickly.

Do not taste any of these samples.
Keep resazurin away from strong sunlight.

a little resazurin solution (made up as directed on the container)
4 test tubes labelled A–D
dropper pipette
beaker half full of warm water
test tube rack (if available)

An equal quantity of milk should be put into each tube (about a quarter the depth of the tube).

In tube A put milk which has been left in a warm room for at least a day and night.
In tube B put the same milk left in a warm room overnight.
In tube C put fresh milk stored in a refrigerator since delivery.
In tube D put fresh milk stored in a refrigerator since delivery (for colour comparison).

1 Draw out a results table into your workbook or folder using these headings, and fill in the first column.

Testing milk for freshness			
Tube letter and contents	Colour of liquid in tube		
	at start	after 30 mins	after 60 mins

2 Add 5 drops of resazurin to tubes A–C.
3 Fill in the second column of the results table. Compare the colours of tubes A–C to that of tube D.
4 Put all the tubes into a beaker of warm water.
5 Write down the results after 30 and 60 minutes.
You can also put these tubes to one side and look for further changes over one or two days as the milk sours.

Questions

1 Which samples changed the colour of the resazurin quickest?
2 Which samples changed the colour most slowly?
3 Which samples had   a the most   b the least bacteria in them?

Further work

1 How should milk be stored?
2 How could you keep milk fresh on a camping holiday?

Tests for vitamin C, starch, and fat

The first two tests should be carried out in an area away from food preparation. Try to predict (guess) the results for each test first.

Testing for vitamin C

This test uses a blue chemical called phenol-indo-2, 6-dichlorophenol. (PIDCP for short, formerly known as DCPIP.)

> a few grains of PIDCP powder dissolved in ¼ beaker cold water (This solution does not keep well so is best if freshly made up. Keep it away from strong sunlight.)
>
> foods to test such as:
>
> | | |
> |---|---|
> | lemonade | orange juice |
> | milk | lemon juice |
> | orange squash | water |
> | canned fruit juice | vegetable cooking water |
>
> test tubes (one for each food)   dropper pipette
> test tube rack, if available

1 Quarter fill each test tube with a different food/drink. Make sure that each tube contains approximately the same amount.
2 Add drops of blue solution one at a time to each food in turn. As you add the blue PIDCP, it reacts with the vitamin C and becomes colourless. When all the vitamin C is used up, the liquid in your tube will look blue. Count the number of drops you add before the blue colour develops. Shake the tubes gently to mix.
3 Keep a careful note of the number of drops needed for each food. If the colour does not change after 25 drops then stop and put 25+ as your result.
4 Write out this table of results into your workbook or folder.

	Testing for vitamin C	
Food/drink	Number of drops of PIDCP needed for blue colour	Is this a *good* source of vitamin C?

5 Remember if there is *little* vitamin C in the food or drink you will only need a *little* PIDCP. Food with *a lot* of vitamin C needs *more* PIDCP before the blue colour develops.

Warning—PIDCP is poisonous so do not taste these foods.

Starch test

Warning—iodine is poisonous and should not be used where food is being prepared.

> testing tiles or saucers
> ¼ teaspoon of flour
> ¼ teaspoon of sugar
> water washed out in preparing gluten (page 29)
> other food samples if wished
> dropper pipette
> iodine solution

1 Put the flour on a testing tile.
2 Add one or two drops of iodine solution. If starch is present the colour will turn **blue/black**.
3 Repeat the test with sugar and with the other foods.
4 When you have finished, wash up the tiles or saucers **away** from the food preparation area. Remember iodine is poisonous.

Test for fat

> foods to be tested
> paper, preferably brown

1 Rub a little of one of the foods on a clean piece of paper.
2 Label this with the name of the food.
3 Repeat with the other foods.
4 Leave for a few minutes until dry.
5 If there is a greasy or translucent (shiny and slightly see-through) mark on the paper then the food contains fat. Foods with only a little fat in may need to be left in contact with the paper for longer.

Questions

1 Copy this chart into your workbook or folder.

Food	Vitamin C	Starch	Fat

2 List all the foods that you have tested in the left-hand column.
3 Fill in the chart.
   Put a √ if the food contained vitamin C, starch or fat.
   Put a ✗ if the food did not contain any or all of these.
   Put a — if the food was not tested.
4 Were your predictions about these foods correct?

Index

acidity 58, 60
additives 20, 21
alkali 58
apple preservation 54

bar chart 13, 14, 18
bias 24
bibliography 10
blanching 54
bran 28
bread 29, 52
butter 38

cakes 48, 49
calculator 9
caramelization 31
carbon dioxide 52
cells 26
cheese 18, 34, 38, 39
coagulation 32–35, 46
colouring 20, 21, 22
conclusions 7
connective tissue 32, 33
control 6
convenience foods 56
cookers 42, 43
cooking methods
  baking 45, 47, 48
  boiling 26, 35
  cakes 48, 49
  grilling 26
costing recipes 9
crisp flavours 23
curdling 47

dairy foods 38
dextrinization 31
dietary fibre 28

eggs 35, 44, 46
egg custard 46
emulsion 36, 37
equipment 40–44
evaluation 11, 42

fat 25, 63
fibre 28
fish 34
flavouring 20, 22, 23
flour 28, 29
foam 44
food choice 16, 17, 25
food labels 20, 22
fractions 14
freshness of milk 61
fruit 16, 20, 22, 54
fruit drinks 23

gelatinization 30
gluten 29

healthy eating 16, 17, 25
health risks 19, 20, 25, 39
heat 28, 30, 32, 34, 46

indicator 58, 59, 60
ingredients 37, 48, 51, 57

labels 20, 23

meat 32, 33
microwave cooker 42, 49
milk 19, 34, 60
mixtures 36

ovens 42, 43

packet foods 20, 21, 23, 56, 57
pastry 50, 51
percentages 14
pH 58, 59, 60
pie chart 13
planning 10
plant cells 26
presentation 11
preservation 54, 55
preservatives 21
prices 15
projects 10, 11, 18, 19, 55
protein 32, 34

recipe costing 9
red cabbage indicator 59
resazurin 60
results 13, 15
results charts 7

safety 6, 13
salad preparation 40
salad dressings 37
school meals 14
shopping 15
snacks 17
solutions 36
starch 30, 31, 63
stock 36
sugar 7, 23, 33, 43
suspension 36
surveys 12, 13, 14, 15, 18, 19

tinned food 20, 21
triangle tests 23

vegetable preparation 27, 40
vegetables 16, 20, 26, 27, 55
vitamin C 62

weighing 8
whisk 44, 45
wholemeal flour 28, 29, 42, 48, 50

yeast 52
yogurt 22, 38, 60